LET'S TALK ABOUT SEX AND LOVING

LET'S TALK ABOUT SEX AND LOVING

Gail Jones Sanchez
with Mary Gerbino

Illustrations by Cynthia Raap

Yes Press
Burlingame, California

Copyright © 1983 by Gail Jones Sanchez and Mary Gerbino
Illustrations copyright © 1983 by Cynthia Raap
ISBN 0-940208-06-7

Yes Press
P. O. Box 2086
Burlingame, California 94010

Additional copies of this book or the other publications of Yes Press can be ordered through your local bookstore or directly from the publisher. (Please add $1.00 for shipping and, if a California resident, 6½% sales tax.)

CONTENTS

HOW TO USE THIS BOOK . . . . Page 5

CHAPTERS

    I   How Do Girls Look Different From Boys? 10
    II What Is Menstruation? What Are Wet Dreams? 20
    III How Do People Make Love? 24
    IV Where Do Babies Come From? 30
    V   When Touching Yourself Feels Good 34
    VI Are You Curious? 36
    VII Who Needs Private Time? 40
    VIII What Are Bathroom Words? 44
    IX When Touching Doesn't Feel Good 48
    X   What Are Adopted and Foster Children? 54
    XI Loving and Feeling Loved 58

GLOSSARY OF TERMS 64

ACKNOWLEDGMENTS

This book is dedicated to Raymond whose love and support is there for me, Myron who is teaching me a lot about children and mothering, and my mother, Essie Jones.

My deep appreciation goes to these people for their influence, direct and indirect, on my writing of this book: Murray Bower, Jean Eaton, Maria Flaherty, Linda Janowitz, Orpha Quadros, and Ada Tal.

Many thanks to all the people who helped with and critiqued the manuscript, especially Diana Colby, Sylvia Cox, Sharon Elliot, Maureen English, Alice Gigax, Beverly Hammel, Holly Ito, Merrill Ito, Jackie Kerns, Judy Maclean, Barbara Martinez, Gary and Sue Plep, Georgia Porcella, Lois Sanchez, Gloria Singer, Rachel Walker, Helen Williams, Joy Yusba, Velita Toff, Joyce Dobbs, Pat McAndrews, and Bunny Carter.

HOW TO USE THIS BOOK

LET'S TALK ABOUT SEX AND LOVING is a book to be read to children by you, their parents. Its intention is to provide a beginning for your discussions. We are not trying to tell you exactly what to say.

You may have been taught, as I was, that it's wrong to talk about sex. Or you may have been given incorrect (or incomplete) information by the people you asked to tell you about it.

For example, I asked a young friend once if she knew what a rubber was. "Of course," she replied. "A rubber is what a man wears when he has his period."

Sex education is a lifelong process which begins at birth. This book will give you information and suggest ways to approach your child with that information. Your own views about sex will influence the way your child receives what you say. Examine your attitudes. Most of us feel awkward or self-conscious about some aspects of sexuality.

A little practice will help. Try talking to your spouse or a friend, or into a tape recorder, before you begin with your child. If this seems difficult at first, consider the benefits to you, your child, and the relationship between you.

HOW TO START

Some parents feel that five to ten-year-old children are too young to learn about sex, especially if their child has not yet begun asking questions about it. But all children in that age group are curious about parts of sexuality! If your child doesn't ask about sex, it may be that he or she has already learned that sex is something to be self-conscious or embarrassed about. If they do not get sex information from you, they will get it elsewhere. Chances are that if this happens, the information they get will be out of line with the truth or your values.

VALUES

Sometimes adults feel uncomfortable about setting limits. But children need limits in all areas of their lives, including sexuality. For example, you may want to stress that sexual intercourse is okay only for married couples. Or you may want your child to feel that any loving or committed relationship can include sexual intimacy. It is up to you to teach your child your values and your definitions of acceptable social behavior.

Asterisks (*) throughout the book indicate places to stop reading and talk to your child about your values. Values are guidelines for setting limits. If you have mixed feelings about some issue it is okay to tell your child that. You might explain what you were taught as a child and then say something about what you have learned since about that subject. Or simply say that not everyone agrees about it, and give a couple of different opinions.

A child learns in bits and pieces. The first time, your child may absorb only one or two things you say. You'll have to go over it again and again. Young children have short attention spans. Perhaps you can begin by looking at the pictures together and reading just one or two pages.

Read this book at a time when you might normally read a storybook to your child. Having a special "sex education" time may embarrass the child and make it hard for him or her to take the information in stride.

As you read, stop periodically and ask your child specific questions to find out what he or she already knows. Listen carefully to your child's answers. This will help you clear up any misconceptions.

Expect questions as you read this book. Children are relaxed about sex, unless they learn from others not to be. Most children have had some kind of sex play with other children by the time they are five years old. If you observe or know about such sex play, be careful not to overreact.

Children become confused about sex because they believe their bodies and feelings are natural, but they are taught inhibitions. We may say to them, "Don't let anyone touch you down there, ever," or, "Don't touch yourself." As adults, they may have difficulty overcoming these inhibitions.

Children hear what you say, but they believe what they see and what they sense you feel about sex. If what you say isn't consistent with your actions, your children will become confused. If you feel that you should talk to your child about masturbation, but you choke up when you do so, your child will sense your embarrassment. Acknowledge your feelings. You can say something like, "I know I seem embarassed by this, but when I was growing up, we didn't talk about sex, so this is really a first time for me, too. Gosh, do I need practice."

Keep your explanations short and to the point. When my niece asked me to tell her about tampons, I made the mistake of launching into a lecture. Fifteen minutes later, she interrupted, "Aunt Gail, I didn't ask for a whole book on sex. I just want to know what a tampon is."

We have said that this book is for children between the ages of five and nine. But you may have a child of four or even three who wants it read to him or her. And we have found ten, eleven and twelve-year-olds who read it with great interest. Children as young as eight may prefer to read the book themselves or with a sibling or friend before discussing the content with you. If so, please respect their choice and do not scold or tease them about any embarrassment or self-consciousness they feel.

CHAPTER I

HOW DO GIRLS LOOK DIFFERENT FROM BOYS?

Some girls and some boys grow tall and thin as forest trees. Some girls and some boys are short and plump as tomato plants. But in one way, the bodies of all girls are different from the bodies of all boys: They have different sex organs. Sex organs are those body parts which tell us whether a baby is a boy or a girl.

The part of a girl's sex organs which we can see is called her vulva. It is between her legs. The vulva has two inner lips and two outer lips. It is soft and cushiony, like cheeks or lips on faces. If you are a girl, you probably have felt your vulva when you took a bath or used the toilet, even if you didn't know the word for it.

The vulva may be the color of a pale pink rose, or a bright red rose, or almost any shade of pink or red. Vulvas, like faces, are all different. It's hard to see your own, but if you use a small mirror, you can look at it.

Tucked inside the inner lips of the vulva are the clitoris and the vagina. The clitoris feels good and tingly when it's touched. Under the clitoris is a tiny opening called the urethra. When urine leaves your body, it comes out through the urethra. The larger opening is called a vagina. Through her vagina, a woman's babies can be born.

Sex organs can also be called genitals. Boys' genitals are different and have different names from girls' genitals. The finger-shaped organ hanging between a boy's legs is called his penis. As a boy grows bigger, his penis grows bigger too, just like his fingers and toes do.

Under a boy's penis hangs the scrotum, which looks like a little sack. Inside the scrotum are two testicles about as big as marbles. When a boy grows into a man, his testicles make millions of sperm cells. Sperm cells are so tiny that there's plenty of room for all of them in a man's testicles.

When boys and girls grow up to be men and women, hair grows all around their genitals. That's one way men and women are the same!

As girls become women, their breasts become larger. Just like noses and lips, breasts on some women are larger than breasts on other women. Breasts produce milk for newborn babies. A newborn baby can't eat apples or chocolate chip cookies or peanut butter sandwiches. Instead, they drink lots of milk.

Men have breasts too, but they don't grow larger or get milk in them. Men don't wear bras. If a man wants to feed a baby some milk, he uses a bottle.

A girl also has sex organs inside her body. She has two ovaries and two tubes. Each ovary is about as big as a jelly bean. When the girl is 9 or 12 or 15, these ovaries begin to produce an egg cell every month. Reaching toward the ovaries, on either side are tiny tubes. These carry the egg cells to the girl's uterus.

The uterus is inside a girl's body, close to her stomach. It's as stretchable as a birthday party balloon. When it's empty, it's about as big as a fist. But when it has a baby growing inside it, the uterus will stretch and stretch as the baby gets bigger. It will fill up with warm liquid so the baby can stay warm and float. The uterus is the perfect place for the baby to stay until it's ready to live outside of its mother's body.

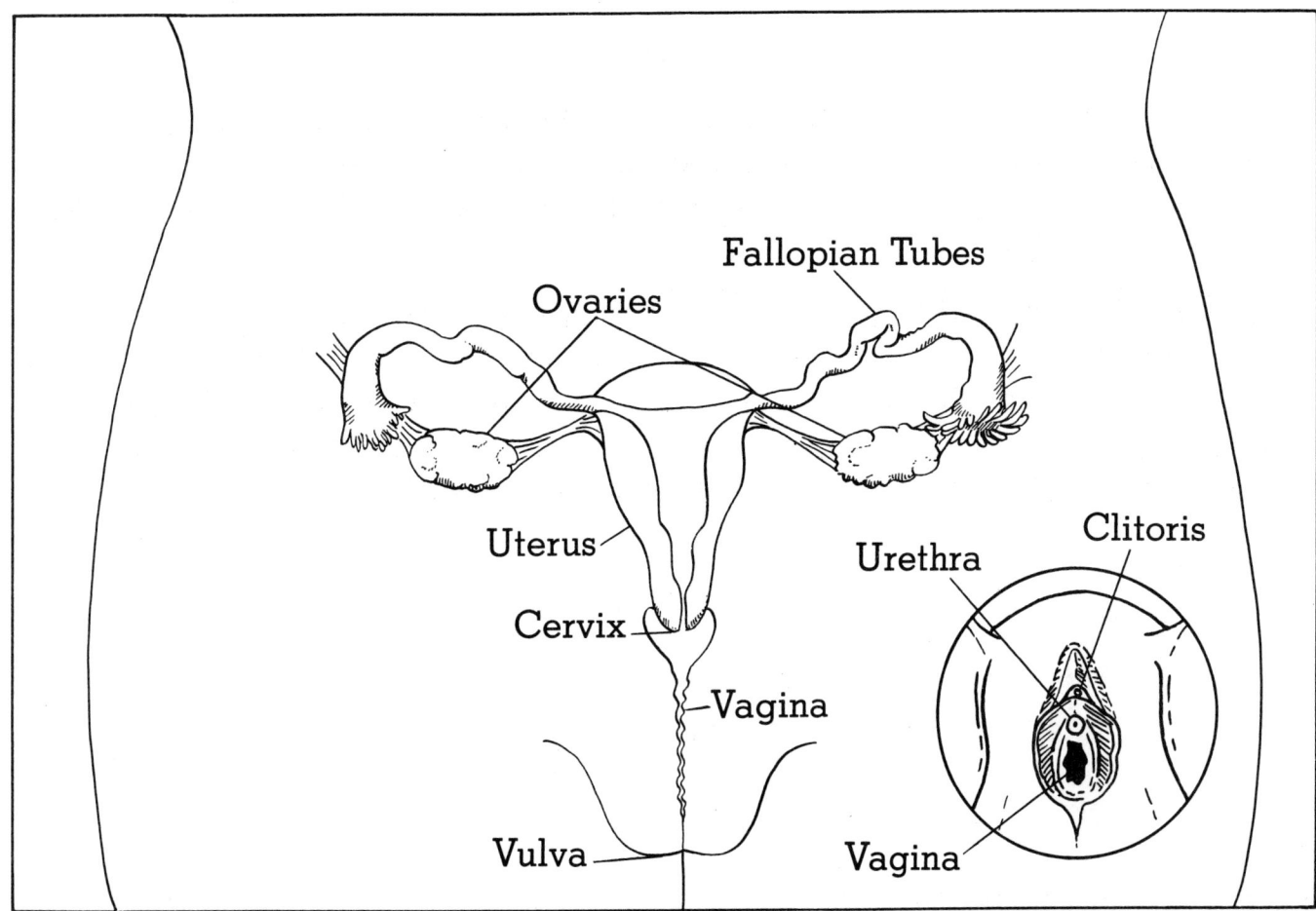

CHAPTER II

WHAT IS MENSTRUATION? WHAT ARE WET DREAMS?

At the same time when a girl's ovaries start making eggs, blood and tissue start to build up in her uterus. This is to shelter and nourish a new baby. When no baby is growing there, the shelter is not needed. Once a month, this blood and tissue drain from her uterus through her vagina. At first it may seem to the girl that a lot of blood and tissue is coming out. But it is not very much: not more than two or three large spoonfuls. It drains out slowly during several days every month, a few drops at a time. The draining is called a menstrual period.

During her period, a girl wears a sanitary pad next to the opening of her vagina, or a tampon, which fits inside her vagina. A pad or a tampon will soak up the menstrual blood when it drains, the way a sponge soaks up water.

A girl can change the napkin or tampon every few hours. Some girls change them whenever they go to the bathroom. You may have wondered about the box of sanitary napkins or tampons in your mother's closet. Ask her to show you one sometime.

When a boy is twelve or thirteen, his body starts making important changes, too. Sperm cells begin to grow in his testicles. These sperm cells live in a thick liquid called semen. Sometimes semen comes out of the end of his penis at night when he's asleep. This is not urine. It is called a wet dream. Many boys have wet dreams.

Although only a spoonful comes out of the end of the boy's penis, the semen can make a large wet spot in his bed, just as a little bit of milk can make a large sticky spot on the floor.

Menstruation and wet dreams, and changing bodies all make it possible for people to share sex, to have children, and to make love with another person.

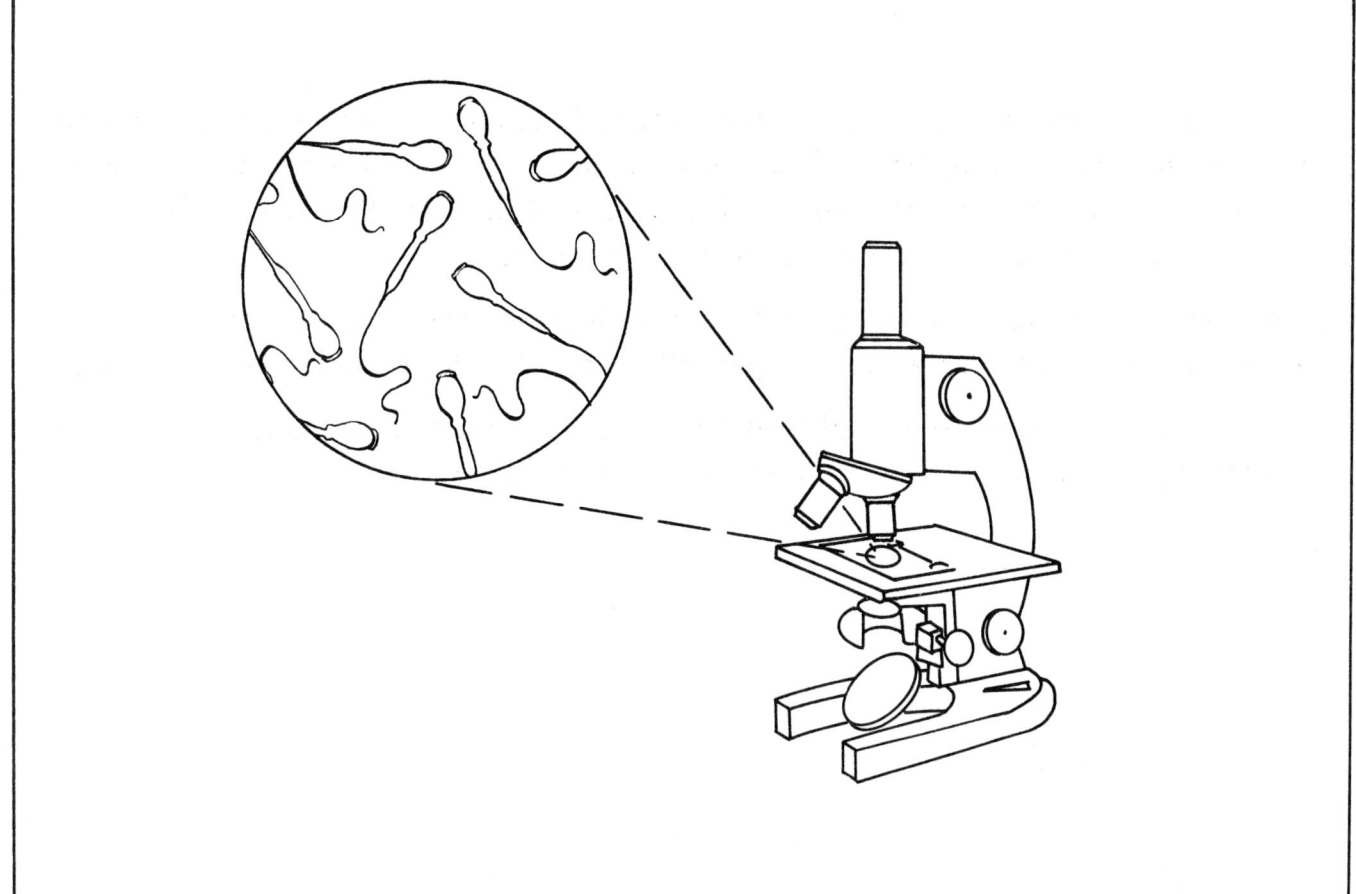

CHAPTER III

HOW DO PEOPLE MAKE LOVE?

Sex is natural, good, and human. People have sexual feelings, whether they are very young or very old, fat, sick, thin, retarded, or in a wheelchair. People can do things that please them sexually. They can laugh, talk, hug, kiss, touch, and have sexual intercourse. All these things are part of making love, but some people mean only sexual intercourse when they say "making love."

Sometimes people have intercourse because they want to make a baby, but mostly they just want to be close and share loving feelings.*

You may be wondering how a man and a woman have sexual intercourse. The man puts his penis inside the woman's vagina. In order to do this, the man's penis must become firm. This is called an erection. During an erection, a man's penis becomes longer and larger. A man or a boy can have an erection because he is thinking about sex, or just because something has touched his penis. In order for the man's penis to slide into the woman's vagina, the woman's vagina must be moist and slippery. This may happen when she thinks about sex or when someone she loves holds her and kisses her.

People can have sexual intercourse in many different positions. One way is for the man to be on top of the woman. When her vagina is moist, she spreads her legs and the man gently puts his penis into her vagina. Another way is for the woman to be on top and put the man's penis inside her vagina. Or they can be lying side-by-side. People can have sexual intercourse in any way that pleases them.

They feel like their whole bodies are kissing.

After the man and the woman have been together for a while, the man or the woman, or both of them may have an orgasm. During an orgasm, their bodies feel warm, excited, and tingly. They want to get very close together. They like the feeling. Sometimes men and women have orgasms when they are touching each other's bodies, even though they are not having intercourse.

An orgasm usually lasts for only a few seconds, but it feels so good that they wish it would continue. It makes them feel warm and full like when you take a big, deep breath and then let it out real fast: WHOOSH! They feel like they are rolled into a ball of good feelings.

An orgasm is like a soap bubble: Every one is different, and none of them lasts very long. Some orgasms are as exciting as ocean waves, and some are quiet as rainbows.

After orgasm, the man's penis becomes soft and his erection goes away. The woman's vagina feels warm and wet. All the tingliness slowly leaves their bodies and they feel content. They feel warm and snuggly, sort of the way you feel when you snuggle up with your teddy bear or blanket.

CHAPTER IV

WHERE DO BABIES COME FROM?

When a man has an orgasm, semen usually comes out of his penis. We call this an ejaculation. The ejaculation is filled with sperm cells. If he ejaculates inside of a woman's vagina, the man's sperm cells rush to meet the egg cell that waits inside the woman's body. If an egg is waiting, it welcomes one of the sperm cells.

The sperm and egg become one, and that means that the egg has been fertilized. From this fertilized egg, a baby will start to grow and grow and GROW.

The baby grows for nine months inside its mother's uterus. It starts out very teeny, smaller than a speck of dust. By the time a baby is ready to be born it will be as big as a watermelon, but not nearly so heavy.

Inside the mother's uterus, the baby wll grow arms and legs, eyes and ears, hair and fingernails, and everything else it needs.

The baby has a special way of getting food from its mother while it is in her uterus. All the food the baby needs comes through the umbilical cord. The umbilical cord is like a soft, flexible tube attached to both the mother and her baby.

The mother can feel it when her baby is ready to be born. The baby will start moving toward the opening of its mother's vagina, and the uterus will squeeze to help push the baby out. The opening of the vagina begins to stretch until it's big enough for the baby's body to fit through. The squeezing of the uterus is called contractions. The work of the woman's body when the baby is getting ready to come out is called labor.

Sometimes the baby can't come out of its mother's vagina because the baby's body is bigger than the opening of the vagina, or for some other reason. If that happens, the doctor makes an opening through the mother's abdomen and reaches inside her uterus to help the baby come out.

Even when the baby comes out of its mother's vagina, someone usually helps the mother with the birth. It might be a nurse and a doctor, or a midwife, or the baby's dad, or another relative or friend. The helper ties and cuts the umbilical cord.

Cutting the umbilical cord doesn't hurt the baby or the mother. When the place where it was tied heals, it becomes a navel. Some people call it a belly-button. Have you ever wondered about your belly-button?

CHAPTER V

WHEN TOUCHING YOURSELF FEELS GOOD

Everyone's body can feel good when it is touched. Doesn't it feel good when your mom or dad hugs you?

If someone like your grandmother, or uncle or friend sees you touching your body, they might get upset or angry. While you're giving yourself warm feelings, they might give you cold looks. Most children touch themselves, but since it makes some people uncomfortable, it's best for you to touch your genitals when you're by yourself, maybe in your room with the door shut.

If someone scolds you for touching yourself, you can say to yourself, "I'm not a bad person. I'm a curious person. I'm just touching my body. I'm exploring. I'm curious."

CHAPTER VI

ARE YOU CURIOUS?

Of course you're curious. Curious means questioning or wondering about something—wanting to know. Probably you're curious about your body and the bodies of other people, too. Boys want to know what other boys and girls look like, and girls want to know what other girls and boys look like. To satisfy this curiosity, sometimes children trade a look at each other.

You may be trading a look with a friend or your brother or sister when someone else sees you. That person might get embarrassed and say something to you about it. If that happens you can say, "There's nothing wrong with being curious! I am not a bad person."

Maybe your mom or dad wishes that you weren't so curious about other peoples' bodies. If they get upset when they see you do it, you could look at the pictures in this book instead. Or you could ask your parents to help you choose some other pictures of peoples' bodies to look at.

Remember, it's not bad or dirty to be curious; it's natural. But don't look at other peoples' bodies unless it is okay with them. When people shut the bathroom or bedroom door while they use the toilet or get dressed, they want privacy. They don't want you to peek under the door or through the keyhole! Most people don't like you to look inside their bathrobes, or hide behind the shower curtain. Everybody deserves privacy and likes private time, just like you do.

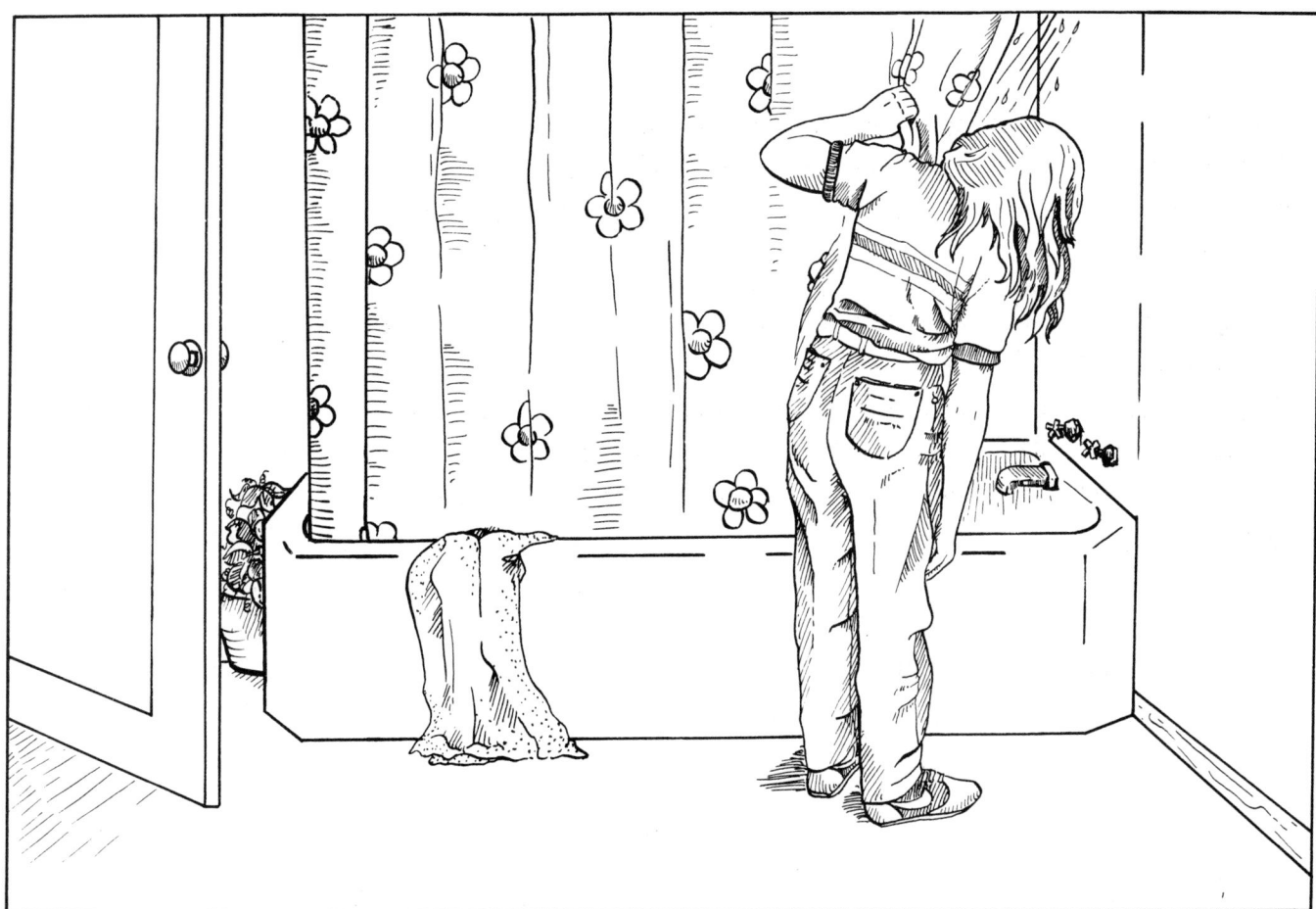

CHAPTER VII

WHO NEEDS PRIVATE TIME?

Everyone needs private time. Private time is spent with yourself alone, to think about anything you like. Maybe you like to spend your private time in your bedroom. If you share your bedroom with someone else, you can still ask for time alone there.

Private time is important. It helps you learn who you are, what you like, and how to grow as a person.

Parents need private time, too. Sometimes they spend their private time in their bedroom, and sometimes they spend it somewhere else in the house. If your parents close the bedroom door and want to be alone, that's not because they want you to feel unloved or left-out. It might be because that's their time to love each other in a private way, or because they just feel like being alone together.

If you want to tell your mom or dad something while they're spending private time, save it and tell them later! They'll be happy to hear it then.

When your parents are spending private time, you can work on a puzzle or look at a book. You can go play with your friends, or you can have your own private time! You can use it as a time to think about new things, play with your toys, or take a nap.

Sometimes when you wake up in the morning, your parents are still asleep. That's another kind of private time that they want to have. Can you find something to do until they wake up? Maybe you could eat some breakfast or make up a game to play.

CHAPTER VIII

WHAT ARE BATHROOM WORDS?

Bathroom words are words that make some adults feel upset. Sometimes they're written on public bathroom walls, or you might hear other people in your neighborhood saying them. Mostly those words make fun of things you do with your body, like bowel movements, urination, and sexual intercourse.

Sometimes you may see or hear a word and not know what it means. The new word may be a bathroom word. If you go home and use this word with members of your family, they may get very upset. Dad might leave the room. Mom might crunch the newspaper in her hand. Your grandmother or grandfather might shake a finger in your face and scold you.

If you hear a new word, find out what it means before you use it. Ask your mom or dad to explain it to you and help you decide if you want to use it.*

If an adult calls you a bad person because you used a bathroom word, you can tell yourself, "I'm not a bad person. I just didn't know what that word meant. I'm learning new words."

It's always exciting to try out new words! But it's important to learn what that new word means, and to know the right time and place to use it.*

If you use bathroom words when you're angry, and you want someone to pay attention to you, the kind of attention you get might not make you feel any better. If you feel angry, you can hit a pillow, or kick a ball, or growl like a dog. And you can tell the person who made you angry, "I'm mad at you."*

If you want some hugs and loving from someone, why don't you ask for that? Then you won't have to use bathroom words to get their attention. Instead, you can ask someone to talk to you or read you a story, or play a game with you, or help you with a project.

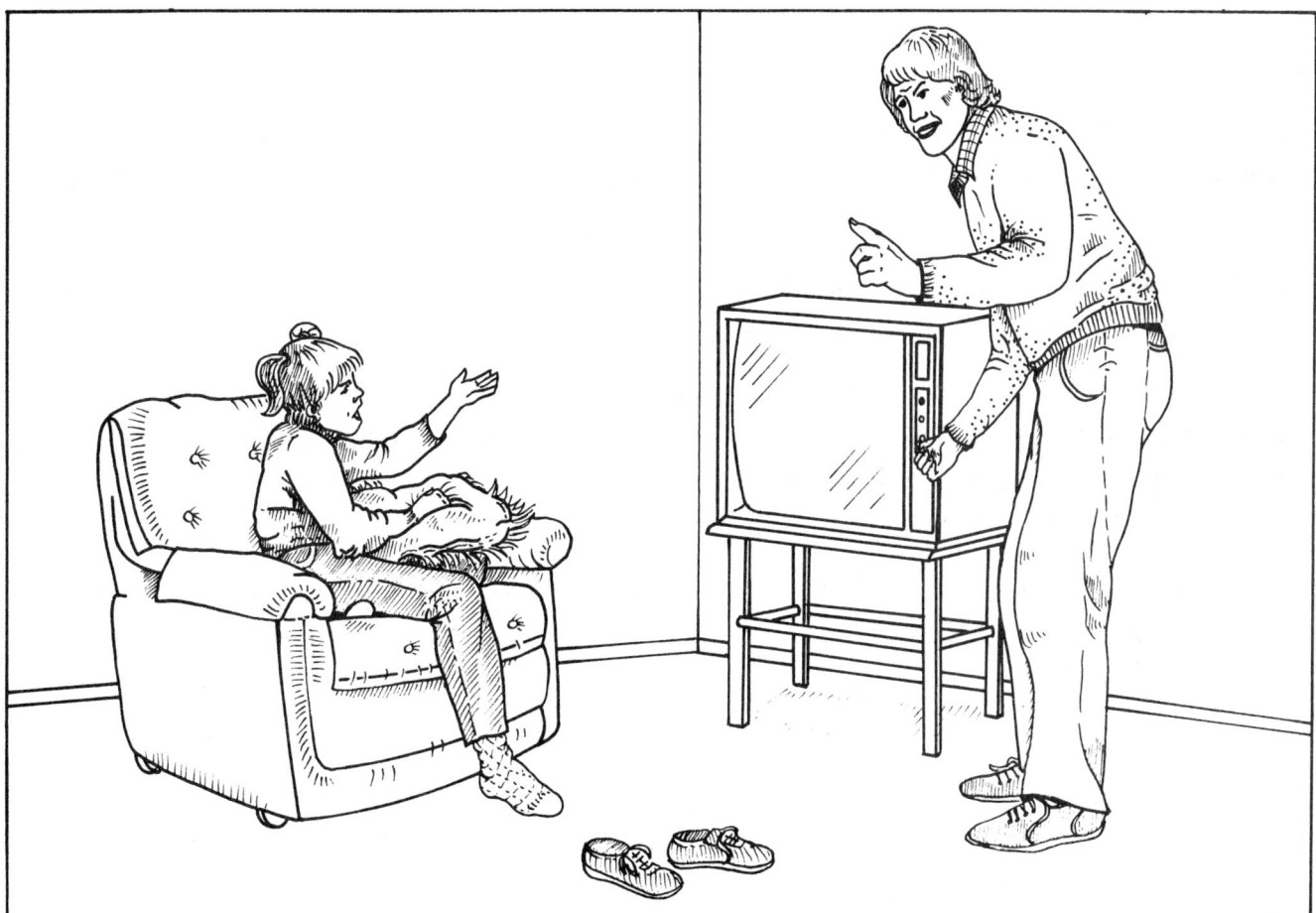

CHAPTER IX

WHEN TOUCHING DOESN'T FEEL GOOD

Sometimes an adult may give you the kind of attention you DON'T want. A friend, a babysitter, or a relative, or someone you don't know, may try to kiss you or touch you in a way that's different from the way other people touch or kiss you. They might want to take off some of your clothing. They might want to look inside your shirt or pull your pants down. DON'T LET THEM DO THIS.

If this happens, you must tell the person to stop what they're doing right now. You can say, "No! Don't do that! I only let my mom or dad help me with my clothes." You have the right to say "No" to adults as well as to other children.

If an adult tries to make you do anything you don't want to do, or something you feel funny about doing, you can say, "No. I won't do that." You can say, "No! Don't touch me!"

Practice saying those words. Say them in a loud, strong voice. Ask your parents to help you practice. How did you do?

Other people don't have the right to look at, or touch, your body if you don't want them to. You deserve privacy just as adults do. You can say NO.

If someone you don't know asks you to get into a car or come into a house, don't get close to that person. Cross the street. If that person follows you, do anything you can to get away. RUN. YELL. Practice now. How loud can you yell?

Don't go near a stranger's car, even if he or she offers to give you some candy, or a puppy or a toy. They might be trying to hurt you.

Can you think of other things strangers might do to try to get you to go with them? Talk about those ways now.*

What if you are walking down the street and you get a funny feeling in your stomach about someone walking near you? Cross the street and stay away from that person. Sometimes stomachs are smarter than heads, so do what your stomach tells you to do.

Don't let other people do things to your body that you don't like, or that make you feel uncomfortable. Don't be afraid to tell your mom or dad, or aunt or uncle, or someone else who cares about you, even if the person who makes you uncomfortable tells you not to tell anyone.

CHAPTER X

WHAT ARE ADOPTED AND FOSTER CHILDREN?

Every baby that's born has a birth mother and a birth father. Every baby was made from the sperm cell of its birth father and the egg cell of its birth mother. But sometimes birth parents can't keep their baby. This might be because the parents are too sick, too young, or too poor. They may decide that even though they love their baby very much and wish they could keep it, it is best to let someone else take care of their child.

Other adults want to have a baby of their own but they can't become birth parents. They choose to take a baby whose birth parents couldn't keep it. They love the baby and raise it as if they were its birth parents. This is called adoption.

Some children live with adults who are not their birth parents, and who have not adopted them. These children live for a few weeks or months in foster homes with foster parents. We call them foster children.

Some foster children live in foster homes because their birth parents are sick or disabled. Once in a while, parents don't know how to take care of their children. Then the children might stay with a foster family for a while. It is not the children's fault that they cannot live with their own parents. Do you know someone who has foster parents?

CHAPTER XI

LOVING AND FEELING LOVED

Loving makes the world a happier place. Would you like a big hug right now? Ask somebody to give you one. Would your mom or dad like a hug right now? Give them one.

Grandparents like hugs, too. So do brothers and sisters and cousins and friends. Pets like to be hugged, especially dogs.

When we share hugs and kisses with people we care about, that's called being affectionate. Being affectionate helps us all feel loved.

Some people didn't get enough affection when they were children. When these people grow up they often don't like others to touch them. They pull away like turtles pulling their heads and feet into their shells. They get as stiff as icicles inside deep caves. They curl their arms around their bodies like prickly vines. They miss the good feelings you and your family get from being affectionate with each other.

There are many ways to show affection. You can make a treat for someone; draw a picture of a sunset or a pony for them. Help them with their chores; sort the silverware, or gather up the garbage. Share your cookies or your books. You can talk to them; tell them you like them. Or just sit quietly together. Learning to give affection and love can fill your days with birdsongs and giggles and buttercups.

It is important to learn about sex because sex is one way for adults to be affectionate and loving with each other. We have already talked about how men and women make love or have sex together. Some people are affectionate and loving with each other but don't have sex together. Some people hardly ever have sex with another person, even though that person is someone they love very much. Some men have loving relationships with other men, and some women have loving relationships with other women.*

You are not old enough to have sex with another person yet, but maybe you have friends who are boys and friends who are girls. You can learn a lot about loving from enjoying times you spend with your friends and your family. Having fun together is one of the best things about loving. And nobody is too young or too old to have fun.

You may have more questions than the ones we've talked about in this book. Ask your parents to tell you what you want to know. They'll find answers for you even if they have to look in some other books.

Now you might be saying, "But I thought parents knew everything already." Parents are people too, just like you; and people are always learning, no matter how young or how old they are. Keep on learning and loving.

GLOSSARY OF TERMS

GLOSSARY OF TERMS

Abdomen: The front part of the body starting under the stomach and going down to the genitals. (Same as "tummy.")

Adopted: Children raised by a mother and father who are not their birth parents.

Affection, affectionate: Touching, holding, hugging, kissing, showing someone that you love them.

Bathroom words: Unacceptable names for bowel movements, urination, genitals and sexual behavior.

Bowel movement: Passing of solid waste material from the body.

Breasts: Front of the chest; in women, used for feeding milk to babies.

Clitoris: Sensitive sex organ of girls and women.

Curious, curiosity: Wanting to know and understand.

Ejaculation: Semen spurting from penis during orgasm.

Erection: Enlargement of the penis because of sexual excitement or because something has touched the penis.

Fallopian Tubes: Passageways that carry egg cells from the ovaries to the uterus.

Fertilized: Joining of sperm cell with egg cell.

Foster: Children who live with another family because their birth parents can't take care of them.

Genitals: All sex organs you can see.

Labor: Stretching and contracting or squeezing of the uterus and vagina during childbirth.

Masturbation: Self-exploration of the genitals.

Menstruation: Blood and tissue passing from the uterus through the vagina each month.

Orgasm: Warm, excited, pleasant feelings in the genital area.

Ovaries: Internal sex organs of girls and women, where egg cells are produced.

Penis: Sensitive sex organ of boys through which semen and urine leave the body.

Privacy: Time alone, not shared with anyone else.

Sanitary napkin: Used to soak up menstrual blood as it leaves the vagina.

Scrotum: Bag of skin holding the testicles.

Semen: Liquid in which sperm live.

Sex Organs: Parts of the body which are used for sex and making babies.

Sexual Intercourse: Putting penis into vagina.

Sperm Cells: Made in the testicles of a man; will start making a baby when joined with the egg cell of a woman.

Tampon: Used to absorb menstrual blood inside the vagina.

Testicles: Where sperm cells are produced.

Umbilical Cord: Feeds baby inside uterus, before it is born.

Urethra: Opening through which urine leaves the body.

Urine: Liquid waste from the body. (Same as "pee.")

Uterus: The place inside a woman where a baby grows before it is born.

Vagina: The opening through which babies can be born.

Vulva: The sex organs of a woman or girl which are on the outside of her body.

Wet Dream: Semen passing out of the penis during sleep.

ABOUT THE AUTHORS

Gail Jones Sanchez is a social worker at Interaction Psychotherapy and Counseling Center in San Jose, California. She received her Master's degree in Social Work from San Jose State University School of Social Work and is an instructor in Human Sexuality at San Jose State University. She received additional sex therapy training at University of California Medical Center in San Francisco. She writes an opinion column for a San Jose area weekly newspaper and has been a guest on TV talk shows. Sanchez is married and is the mother of one child.

Mary Gerbino is a freelance writer whose many published articles have focused on children and education. She has been honored as an Achiever by American Pen Women; in 1979 she received the West Santa Clara County School Administrators Association Award for outstanding service to education in the media. Gerbino has ten years experience teaching weekly religious education classes, and is the mother of two sons.

TWO MORE BOOKS FOR CHILDREN FROM YES PRESS

The Playbook for Kids About Sex by Joani Blank, Illustrations by Marcia Quackenbush

This play/workbook encourages children to express their sexual self-awareness through writing and drawing pictures. The Playbook focuses on the non-reproductive aspects of sex, and makes no value judgments about sexual choices. Designed for children ages 7 and up, it makes a great gift for parents or friends of young children.

$4.75

A Kid's First Book About Sex by Joani Blank, Illustrations by Marcia Quackenbush

This book offers the same information as *The Playbook for Kids About Sex* in a re-useable, non-workbook format. Lots of new illustrations have been added, making *A Kid's First Book About Sex* as lively and fun to read as its predecessor.

$5.50

To order these books, or to obtain additional copies of *Let's Talk About Sex and Loving*, please use the order form provided. Contact the publisher for quantity discount information.

ORDER FORM

QUANTITY	TITLE	PRICE
	Let's Talk About Sex and Loving	$6.00
	The Playbook for Kids About Sex	$4.75
	A Kid's First Book About Sex	$5.50
Please add $1.25 to your order for postage and handling.		SHIPPING
Enclose payment in full with your order.		TOTAL

NAME _____

ADDRESS _____

Mastercard/Visa Number _____ Expiration Date _____

Yes Press   **P. O. Box 2086**   **Burlingame, CA 94010**